—Books by Harold Jaffe—

Infected Desert (documentary poems)
Kafka Kafka (bio, docufictions)
Single-Sentence Stories (with Tom Whalen)
Sacrifice (fictions & Docufictions)
Brando Bleeds (novel)
Strange Fruit & Other Plays
Performances for The End of Time
BRUT: Writings on Art & Artists
Porn-anti-Porn
Goosestep (fictions & docufictions)
Sacred Outcast: Dispatches from India
Death Café (fictions & docufictions)
Induced Coma: 50 & 100-Word Stories
Othello Blues (novel)
Revolutionary Brain (essays & quasi-essays)
OD (docufictions)
Paris 60 (travel, docufictions)
Anti-Twitter: 150 50-Word Stories
Jesus Coyote (novel)
Beyond the Techno-Cave: A Guerrilla Writer's Guide to Post-Millennial Culture (non-fiction)
Terror-Dot-Gov (docufictions)
15 Serial Killers (docufictions; visuals by Joel Lipman)
Son of Sam (docufiction)
Nazis, Sharks & Serial Killers (non-fiction)
False Positive (docufictions)
Sex for the Millennium (extreme tales)
Straight Razor (stories; visuals by Norman Conquest)
Othello Blues (novel)
Eros Anti-Eros (fictions)
Madonna and Other Spectacles (fictions)
Beasts (fictions)
Mourning Crazy Horse (fictions)
Dos Indios (novel)
Mole's Pity (novel)

THE INFECTED DESERT

Israel at War with the Palestinians

Documentary Poems
by Harold Jaffe

JEF Books / Journal of Experimental Fiction / Depth Charge
Arlington Heights, Illinois

Copyright © 2024 by Harold Jaffe

ISBN 978-1-884097-59-1

ISSN 1084-547X

Front cover design by Norman Conquest

JEF 102

The foremost in innovative fiction
www.experimentalfiction.com

The primary inspiration for my volume is *Zero Hour*, the socially engaged book of documentary poems by the Sandinista poet-priest Ernesto Cardenal, 1980.

CONTENTS

Children of Gaza ...9
Humanness ...10
Bernie ...11
International Outrage ...12
International Outrage ...13
Feeding the Children ...14
Untitled ...16
Israeli Prisons ...17
History ...18
Lavender ... 19
Rules of Engagement ... 20
Never Again ...22
Ultra-Orthodox ...23
Untitled ...24
Mein Kampf ...25
Bound and Buried ...26
Amnesia ...27
Rational Nihilism ...28
Weaponizing the Holocaust ...30
Like a Lynching ...31
Never Again ...32
Contagion ...33
Khan Younis ...34
Marketing of Automatic Murder ...35
Rafah ...36

Fingernails ...37
Man-Made Starvation ...38
Pegasus ...39
Israeli Settlers ...40
Roundup ...41
Exact a Price ...43
The Day After ...44
War but No War ...45
Back & Forth With Lies ...46
Iran vs Israel ...47
Never Again ...48
Artists ...49
My Heart ...50
White Phosphorus ...51
Impunity ...52
Israel Strikes Back ...54
Quantum ...55
International Activists ...56
The Issue for Israel ...58
Terrorist Monsters ...59
About Two Hours North ...60
Untitled ...62
World Court ...64
Two Surprise Assaults ...65
Pariah ...66
The Samson Option ...67

"Oh people of the world, what is happening is wrong! Have mercy on us! Stop the war! Stop the war! Children are dying in the streets!"
a Palestinian man cried inside the bombed hospital.

CHILDREN OF GAZA*

Who will judge them, these powerful governments and leaders, whose neglectful, hypocritical and self-interested policies combined to produce this tragedy?

No judgment. Official lies. Political amnesia.

And who will judge you, in whose name these governments fail to act?

"You" will forget or lie to yourself.

Answer: the children of Gaza. Their judgment and their revenge will be unsparing, indiscriminate, terrible.

Can we assume the world itself survives with "meat humans" rather than the meatless bones of AI bots?

---

*The non-italicized portions were written by Simon Tisdall, of the Guardian; the italicized portions are my "interventions."

HUMANNESS

Even among Israelis who want to stop fighting, it is the bloody endlessness of the war that disturbs them.

I saw a photo of an Israeli woman with a large sign that read: HALF A YEAR OF HELL, but she meant hell for Israelis not the thousands of murdered Palestinians.

I've never heard or read a single Israeli word about the humanness of the Palestinians, who love their children and plant vegetable gardens in the resistant desert, and in fact often resemble Israelis physically.

BERNIE

The Vermont senator and former US presidential hopeful Bernie Sanders told the prime minister of Israel, Benjamin Netanyahu: "Stop murdering innocent people."

Sanders delivered his blunt message in an interview with MSNBC on Tuesday, a day after seven aid workers were killed by an Israeli airstrike in Gaza.

"Stop murdering innocent people," Sanders said.
"Two-thirds of the over 32,000 people killed [in Gaza] are women and children. This is inexcusable."

But not to Bibi Netanyahu who will not heed advice from the democratic socialist senator, who is Jewish but anti-Semitic, in Netanyahu's view.

INTERNATIONAL OUTRAGE

When I remarked that Israel is likely to dismiss international outrage over its genocide of Palestinians because Jews have been despised and persecuted throughout western history, the man, with his thin legs crossed, sipping white wine, responded:

"Maybe there was reason for Jews to be despised."

His response was casual, offhand, but it stung.

INTERNATIONAL OUTRAGE

Despised and persecuted throughout western history, capped by the Holocaust which killed millions, many Israeli Jews have contempt for so-called international outrage even if it means slaughtering innocent people who resemble them.
 What can that signify?

An indirect display of the oft-repeated Jewish Self-Hatred?

FEEDING THE CHILDREN

Seven aid workers trying to deliver much-needed food to Gaza were killed in an Israeli strike in the city of Deir al-Balah on Monday night. The Israeli government confirmed its military had carried out "an unintended strike," hours after World Central Kitchen (WCK), an international charity that has brought hundreds of tons of food aid into Gaza, claimed the IDF was responsible.

WCK said the workers--three Britons, a Palestinian, a US-Canadian, a Pole and an Australian--had been travelling in two armored cars bearing the charity's logo.
       Despite coordinating movements with the IDF, the convoy was hit as it was leaving the Deir al-Balah warehouse, where the team had unloaded more than 100 tons of humanitarian food aid brought to Gaza on the maritime route. IDF sources told Haaretz that the aid workers' vehicles had been hit three times because of suspicions that a terrorist was travelling with the convoy.

Some of the passengers left their vehicle
       after it was hit by the first missile and climbed into another car,
       which was then hit by a second missile.
The third car in the convoy, which approached to pick up

the occupants of the second car,
>> **was hit by a third missile.**

The strike killed all of the WCK workers in the convoy.

Benjamin Netanyahu: *"This happens in war. We are thoroughly looking into it …"*

UNTITLED

The Canadian doctor was making her rounds of the intensive care unit on her final day at the battered public hospital in southern Gaza when she stopped next to two young arrivals with facial injuries and breathing tubes in their windpipes.

The nurse said they were brought in a couple of hours ago. They had sniper shots to the brain. Seven or eight years old.

The Canadian doctor's heart sank. These were not the first children targeted by Israeli snipers, and she knew the damage a single high-caliber bullet could do to a fragile young body.

"They were unable to talk, paraplegic. They were lying like vegetables. They were not the only ones," she whispered. "They were not the only ones. I saw small children with direct sniper shot wounds to the head as well as in the chest."

According to the Palestinian health ministry, children account for more than one in three of the more than 32,000 people killed in Israel's months-long assault on Gaza.

ISRAELI PRISONS

We've heard endless patter about the Israeli "hostages," which Netanyahu has been cynically manipulating.
We've heard almost nothing about the estimated 10,000 Palestinians in Israeli prisons, many for years, some tortured, more than a third held without charge, containing women and children as young as 12-years-old.

HISTORY

The US discovered a country that was already inhabited by a wiser, kinder, more integrated people that the US abused in multiple ways—murdering, force-marching away from their ancestral lands, force-feeding Christianity . . .

>That was a long time ago and (political) history is amnesia.

Are we to be surprised that the US would discount the millions of Palestinians whose lands are violently usurped by the "nation-state" of Israel?

LAVENDER

The Israeli military's bombing campaign in Gaza has employed an AI-powered database that at one stage identified 37,000 potential targets based on their often tangential links to Hamas.

Using rapid readouts of their AI system, called Lavender, Israeli intel officials selected large numbers of Palestinian civilians to be exterminated.

"This is unparalleled," said one officer who used Lavender, adding that the IDF had more faith in a "statistical mechanism" than a grieving Palestinian. "The machine did it coldly, which made it easier."

Another IDF Lavender user, questioned about humans' roles in the selection process, said: "The machine is reliable enough for our purposes."

Developed by the Israel Defense Forces' elite intelligence division, Unit 8200, Lavender marks humans via their use on social media or their alleged contacts with "suspicious" Arabs or their use of a word or phrase, and adds them to a "kill list."

For its part, Hamas uses guerrilla warfare and claims that two Hamas fighters are born for everyone who is "martyred."

RULES OF ENGAGEMENT

The killing of seven foreign aid workers in Gaza has once again raised questions about the IDF's opaque and highly permissive rules of engagement, whether those rules are enforced, and how willing the IDF is to investigate breaches.

Put simply, rules of engagement define how and in what circumstances it is permissible to use force, including lethal violence, and at what potential risk to civilians.

Even though Israel has promised a full and professional investigation into the killing of the aid workers from World Central Kitchen, human rights organizations have long raised questions about the IDF's rules, amid allegations that the ones that do exist are being ignored by soldiers and commanders on the ground.

While soldiers on the ground are allegedly advised when to use lethal force against nearby individuals on the loosely defined risk posed by proximity, the more serious issue in terms of civilian casualties has been the application of so-called "operational modes."

In previous conflicts, the IDF is believed to have broadly applied three levels of operational mode--from most restrictive to most permissive, which specify an acceptable level of damage to structures and a permissible ratio of civilian casualties, in relation to the value of the target.

In the current war, rules that were already permissive in previous conflicts in Gaza have been loosened further, as evidenced by the number of civilian casualties in high-profile strikes. In previous outbreaks of fighting, women and children have made up roughly a third of fatalities.

In this conflict, the proportion appears to be between 60% and 70%-- a far higher civilian-combatant ratio.

The sheer number of strikes that have occurred during the six-month war also raises questions of how detailed the intelligence behind them can be given the persistent concerns over the Israeli use of AI to identify targets.

What that tolerance means in practical terms was described pithily in an investigation by the progressive Israeli newspaper Haaretz: "In Gaza, everyone does as he pleases, where those killed, civilian or otherwise," are defined by default as being "terrorists."

NEVER AGAIN

Their deathskull is not stuffed with golden hair.
They look like your Semitic twin.
Even though you murder them with technology,
they will escape and be reborn in their caves and tunnels,
in their blown apart hospitals,
      And your dream of forever more *Lebensraum*
will never be realized so long as the black
raptor-turned-cannibal   circles circles.

ULTRA-ORTHODOX

I will never enter the army.

Studying the Torah is everything.

We live by the word of God.

We will follow the directions of our rabbis.

Studying the Torah is the only way for us to kill the Arabs.

UNTITLED

If their wrists are amputated because of the iron cuffs
they wear 24 hours a day, that's the way it is.

If they shit in diapers, that's the way it is.

We have thousands of terrorist prisoners.
If they die, it's less work for us.

Does it matter that they were civilians not directly connected to
Hamas or other terrorist groups? No, it doesn't.

MEIN KAMPF

What we will do to our enemies in the coming days and weeks will reverberate for generations, he said.

For every Israeli hostage that Hamas murders, we will murder 900 Arab prisoners, he said.

They say I "played" the so-called Israel lover Joe Biden, he said.

US presidents are weak and stupid, and Obama was weak, stupid and African, he said.

Iran, Lebanon, Yemen—maybe Russia and the rest of Europe—let them all get involved, he said.

They say international opinion has turned against Israel; that is nothing new, he said.

We don't forget that international opinion, even including our "friends," the Americans, refused to intervene in the Holocaust, he said.

If you think I welcome this war to ensure my own political survival, that is a lie, he said.

My son is in Florida, not with the IDF, he said.

BOUND AND BURIED

Palestinian civil defense teams began exhuming bodies from a mass grave outside the Nasser hospital complex in Khan Younis last week after Israeli troops withdrew.

"We feel the need to raise the alarm because there have been multiple bodies discovered," said Ravina Shamdasani, spokesperson for the UN high commissioner for human rights.

She described bodies "buried deep in the ground and covered with waste," adding that "among the deceased were older people, women and wounded," including bodies bound and stripped of their clothes.

"Some had their hands tied, which indicates serious violations of international human rights law and international humanitarian law, and these need to be subjected to further investigations," she said.

The IDF denies any wrongdoing.

AMNESIA

History becomes amnesia so that world leaders make the same grievous mistakes and profit from it.
How long has it been since American students protested against the US war in Vietnam, with thousands of young men escaping conscription and others jailed?

Half a century and millions of deaths later, wise heads concede that the ethnocide in Vietnam and Cambodia was unjust.

Since Vietnam there have been too many US wars and quasi-wars to count, but the Israel-Palestinian war has touched a vein for several reasons, notably the "Jewish question," and the "weaponization" of the Holocaust, which was the prime incentive for Jews to "found" their own country.

As before, conscionable college students and others are silenced or prosecuted for objecting to poor people being massacred even as the US is mindlessly complicit.

RATIONAL NIHILISM

On Sunday, February 25, Aaron Bushnell, a US Air Force serviceman, immolated himself outside the Israeli embassy in Washington, DC, in protest of Israel's ongoing war on Gaza and US support for it. Like many other young people around the United States, Bushnell had been inundated with brutal images, videos, and stories coming out of Gaza—residential blocks leveled, hospital patients massacred, hungry Palestinians shot dead trying to get access to aid.

Two days after Bushnell's death, some voters in Michigan's Democratic primary engaged in a more prosaic act of dissent. They organized a movement to vote "uncommitted" in the Democratic presidential primary. The effort won over 100,000 votes, 13 percent of the primary vote share.

Since then, grassroots efforts in other states to vote uncommitted have followed Michigan's lead.

The movement to vote uncommitted, like Bushnell's suicide, is a manifestation of widespread desperation and exhaustion. Americans who see the need to end Israel's war on Gaza do not have a presidential candidate or political party to vote for. The normal political avenues for expressing disgust with Israel's war and US complicity have been blocked. After countless emails and calls to congresspeople, mass street protests, and civil disobedience, the images of wholesale starvation and slaughter keep beaming through our phones.

Though the uncommitted vote counts are impressive, they are also a reflection of the bind facing antiwar forces. The most compelling option in this presidential primary is to vote for no one.

Our political institutions seem rigidly unresponsive to progressive demands in general, not just disapproval of the war in Gaza. Despite years of protest, there has been no meaningful action on climate change, economic inequality, or mass incarceration. If Democrats continue to dismiss or ignore nonviolent protest as well as attempts to register dissent at the ballot box, would it be a surprise to witness more young people resorting--as Bushnell did--to drastic and violent measures?

The reality is that deepening feelings of political nihilism are a rational response to the disheartening political conditions.

Harold Jaffe

WEAPONIZING THE HOLOCAUST

About the university protests throughout the US, Netanyahu predictably recalled Nazi Germany in the 1930s and angrily counseled students to cease their "antisemitism" and get back in school.

During the Vietnam war, student protesters were accused of excess "enthusiasm," and lacking "reason," but the philosopher Norman Brown pointed out that "enthusiasm" comes from the Greek "en theos," having God inside.

Not pallid liberalism, but enthusiasm, which approaches "sublime madness" in Reinhold Niebuhr's phrase, is in fact eminently "rational" in response to the slaughtering of Palestinians.

LIKE A LYNCHING

Inevitably, rightwing non-student self-appointed vigilantes, violent and masked, have infiltrated the protests, either pretending to be Jews, whom they hate or Muslims, whom they hate.

Sometimes, the vigilantes are unmasked, white faces aflame, shouting obscenely provocative slogans, beating actual protesters, sowing chaos while the police keep out of the way.

As at a lynching, they are to be expected. There are hundreds of violent American hate groups and the number is rising, according to the Southern Poverty Law Center.

Harold Jaffe

NEVER AGAIN

You are Jewish but not Israeli.

You lament the Holocaust and are still furious that except for the Warsaw uprising the Jews went meekly.

Those unkilled, with good riddance from Europe, founded their own country that in fact was inhabited by nearly a million Palestinians.

The Jews' familiar "Never Again" applies to the Nazis, the pogroms, and Jew-hating confreres throughout the world.

Never Again is misapplied to the Palestinians who are primarily Semitic brothers and sisters to the Israelis forced together and apart by the fatal ironies of desperation, hate, and poverty.

CONTAGION

Where are the Israeli equivalents of Nadine Gordimer, Andre Brink, Athol Fugard, JM Coetzee--the white writers in South Africa who wrote and spoke out unequivocally against apartheid?

Where is Peace Now? Or has all of Israel bought in to the massacre of Palestinians?

Did they "buy in" or is it an emotional contagion that is virtually inescapable?

KHAN YOUNIS

"In every house there is a martyr. Words cannot describe the devastation and the suffering we experienced. We cried hysterically at the sight of the blood."

Muhammad Abu Diab said: "There is nothing left. I cannot bear the sight. I'm going to look in the rubble until I find clothes to wear. I'll go back and live next to the rubble of my house even if it's in a tent"

Ahmad Abu al-Rish said: "It's all just rubble. Animals can't live here, so how is a human supposed to?"

Israel's sudden retreat from Khan Younis and the wider south has confounded the Israeli hawks.

The ultra-right ministers who want to press on to Rafah vow that a retreat will mark the end for the prime minister.

MARKETING OF AUTOMATED MURDER

Turkey's state-run news agency reports that the IDF is using Gaza as a weapons-testing site for Lavender, its AI state of-the-art electronic tool which has been responsible for thousands of indiscriminate killings in Gaza and the West Bank, so that Israel can market the tools as battle-tested.

It has been called the "marketing of automated murder."

RAFAH

Everyone in Rafah is living in absolute desperation and fear of what is about to happen.

Thousands and thousands of people so close together.

No water supplies, lakes of raw sewage everywhere.

Children—toddlers--squatting by the roadside with pans begging for food.

FINGERNAILS

As expected, the other shoe dropped and Israel is invading Rafah both in the air and on the ground allegedly to erase Hamas once and for all.

About Biden's warning that the US would not supply armaments to an invasion of Rafah, Netanyahu shrugged it off, declaring that Israel will fight alone, with its "fingernails," if necessary.

Of course, Netanyahu knows that Biden will "walk back" his solemn promise not to supply armaments and continue contributing mindlessly to the slaughter of Palestinians.

After days and nights of bombing, a UN spokesperson said that more than 150,000 thousand Palestinians are fleeing Rafah, many of whom had fled many times before, and they are "exhausted, degraded, humiliated."

MAN-MADE STARVATION

The surge in aid into Gaza that Benjamin Netanyahu promised Joe Biden a week ago has not materialized, as famine is taking hold in the besieged coastal strip.

The increase in the number of aid truck crossings into Gaza claimed by Israel conflicts with UN records and already appears to be faltering.

Another of Netanyahu's pledges to Biden, to open the Ashdod port north of Gaza as a portal to sea-borne humanitarian aid, has led to no action. Two other steps Israel was supposed to take to increase the flow of assistance are allegedly under way, but with no target completion date.

On Wednesday, Samantha Power, head of USAID, became the first American official to confirm publicly that famine had already got a grip in north Gaza.

"Famine is already occurring there?" she was asked

"Yes," she replied.

PEGASUS

Why is Israel's Pegasus so dangerous?

It can be planted secretly, giving the attacker total control over a victim's mobile phone whether on or off. It undermines all the modern security features like encryption and turns a smartphone into a smart listening device. It can also copy messages, photos, and emails as well as recording calls.

How is Pegasus tested?

On live Palestinian subjects.

Why is Pegasus more dangerous than other spyware?

Pegasus was used against the inner circle of dissident Saudi journalist Jamal Khashoggi, murdered and dismembered by Saudi intelligence in 2018. Reports have also revealed the use of Pegasus against journalists, activists, and political dissidents in various countries. The spyware has facilitated assassinations and severe human rights violations by authoritarian regimes in the Middle East and South America.

ISRAELI SETTLERS

Dozens of enraged Israeli settlers, searching for a missing 12-year-old autistic boy from their settlement, stormed into a Palestinian village in the Israeli-occupied West Bank shooting and setting houses and cars on fire.

One Palestinian man was killed and 25 others were wounded in the attack. The deceased man was later identified as 26-year-old Jehad Abu Alia. "My son went with others to defend our land and honor and this is what happened," Afif Abu Alia said from a hospital in the West Bank city of Ramallah, where his son's corpse had been transported.

Palestinian health officials say more than 460 Palestinians have been killed in the West Bank by Israeli forces since the war erupted in October.

The missing 12-year-old Israeli was later found; he had gotten lost in the desert.

ROUNDUP

THE US: Joe Biden is stubborn and mindless and has misread public opinion and the presidential polls.

THE UK: Rishi Sunak has no interest in the Middle East and is happy to play the Tony Blair lapdog role.

INSTITUTIONAL GERMANY: everlasting guilt about the Holocaust which Israel reinforces whenever it senses a deviation.

FRANCE: As always France wants to show the world that it is going its own way but doesn't have the nerve to seize opportunities.

CANADA: Trudeau is vain, a bit simple-minded, and looks to his French-speaking colleague Macron to pave a way.

RUSSIA: Putin, mostly caught up with the Ukraine war, is always looking for openings in the Middle East but seems satisfied with the carnage for the time being.

THE EASTERN EUROPEAN BLOC: Absorbed with their own problems and anxieties about Russia.

CHINA: Busy courting the wealthy Arab countries with a sharp eye on the Israel-Palestinian conflict.

INDIA: Previously pro-Palestine, but under Muslim-hater Narendra Modi, they've changed course and been rewarded with spyware and munitions from Israel.

SAUDI ARABIA AND THE EMIRATES: mouthing support for the Palestinians but in fact consumed with Israeli spyware and electronic intel to deal with their own enemies.

IRELAND: Independent-minded and typically ethical in foreign affairs.

SPAIN AND THE NORDIC COUNTRIES: Will mostly follow Ireland's lead. But not Finland who is scared of the Big Bear.

EXACT A PRICE

Israel will exact a price
      Exact a price
from Iran in response to its mass missile and drone attack when the time is right, war cabinet minister Benny Gantz declared.

"We will exact the price
      Exact the price
From Iran in the fashion and timing that is right for us," Gantz said as the Israeli war cabinet was due to convene to discuss Israel's response.

The Iranian government earlier hailed its unprecedented direct strike on Israel and said that as far as it was concerned the military operation was over, insisting it had struck the intended military targets as a reprisal for the Israeli assault on Iran's consulate in Damascus on April 1.

An Israel Defense Forces spokesperson disagreed insisting that 99% of the more than 300 missiles and drones were intercepted from Iran's attack (thanks to the intervention of the US, UK, France, and Jordan.)

THE DAY AFTER

Israel is being severely criticized by several of its own intel people for acting precipitously without regard to circumstance. According to critics, in the immediate aftermath of October 7, Israel rushed headfirst into what has proven to be a messy, genocidal campaign in Gaza, with no clear notion of "the day after."

Their "genocide" of Gaza civilians and murder of foreign aid workers have been unconscionable, and most recently their bombing of the Iranian embassy in Damascus was reckless. Now they are considering broadening the war not only to the powerful Hezbollah in Lebanon, but to Iran itself.

The IDF, primarily comprised of army reservists, is obviously depending on continuing US and UK support, despite Biden's promise not to stand by Israel if it attacks Iran.

WAR BUT NO WAR

The "regional" war in the Middle East now involves at least 16 countries and includes first strikes from Iranian territory on Israel, but the United States continues to insist continues to insist there is no broader war, lying about the extent of American military involvement. Yet in response to Iran's attack, the U.S. flew aircraft and launched air defense missiles from at least eight countries, while Iran and its proxies fired weapons from Iraq, Syria, and Yemen.

BACK & FORTH WITH LIES

Turkish, Jordanian and Iraqi officials said that Iran gave notice before its attack.
U.S. officials said Iran did not warn Washington.
Iran launched hundreds of drones and missiles in a retaliatory attack after an Israeli strike on its embassy in Syria.
Most of the drones and missiles were downed before reaching Israeli territory.
Iran said their reaction was a response to Israel's attack on its embassy in Damascus and that it would not go beyond this.
Iran sent the United States a message only after the strikes began, said a Biden official.
The official added that Iran's claim of widespread warning was probably an attempt to compensate for the lack of major damage from the attack.
US officials said they had expected an imminent attack and urged Iran against it.
Biden remarked pridefully that his only message to Iran was: "Don't."
How far escalation can be avoided remains in question.
Biden told Israel the US will not join any Israeli retaliation.
Can he be believed?
Israel is weighing its options.

IRAN vs ISRAEL

**Benjamin Netanyahu is seeking
to trap
the West into a total war across the
Middle East that would have incalculable
consequences for the region and the world,
Iran's top diplomat in the UK has claimed
in his first interview since Tehran launched
an unprecedented missile and drone attack
against Israel.**

"The response to the next mistake of the Zionist will not take 12 days' time.
It will be decided soon as we see what the hostile regime has done.
It will be immediate, without warning.
It will be stronger and more severe."
He ruled out Iran attacking civilian centers or nuclear sites.

NEVER AGAIN

Netanyahu's office thanked the various international intercessors for their support, but told them: "We will make our own decisions, and the State of Israel will do everything necessary to defend itself."

So Bibi is prepared to wage a multi-front war against Hamas, Hezbollah, and Iran, armed with Israeli army reservists and AI. But not alone, counting on support from the US, UK, and other European nations.

Does Netanyahu know what he's doing or is it the ubiquitous NEVER AGAIN—misapplied?

ARTISTS

The artists and curators of the Israeli national pavilion at the Venice Biennale have announced their decision not to open until "a ceasefire and hostage release agreement are reached" in the Gaza conflict.

An open letter signed by nearly 25,000 artists had previously called for the "deplatforming" of the Israel pavilion, citing the ban preventing apartheid South Africa from participating in the Venice Biennale between 1968 and 1993.

One Israeli artist said "There is no end in sight, only more pain, loss and devastation. The art can wait but the women and children cannot."

Palestinian artists are represented through a "collateral event" titled South West Bank, and one of the Palestinian artists in the "collateral event" said: "A ceasefire and the release of hostages may mean business as usual for the Israeli pavilion, but for us it is a continuation of 75 years of occupation and apartheid. We are not just fighting for a ceasefire in 2024 but for our liberation."

HAROLD JAFFE

MY HEART

When an Israeli shell struck Gaza's largest fertility clinic in December, the explosion blasted the lids off five liquid nitrogen tanks stored in the embryology unit. As the ultra-cold liquid evaporated, the temperature inside the tanks rose, destroying more than 4,000 embryos plus 1,000 more specimens of sperm and unfertilized eggs stored at Gaza City's Al Basma IVF center.

The impact of that single explosion was far-reaching--an example of the unseen toll Israel's six-and-a-half-month-old assault has had on the 2.3 million people of Gaza. The embryos in those tanks were the last hope for hundreds of Palestinian couples facing infertility.

"We know deeply what these 5,000 lives, or potential lives, meant for the parents," said Bahaeldeen Ghalayini, the obstetrician who established the clinic in 1997.

"At least half of the couples--those who can no longer produce sperm or eggs to make viable embryos--will not have another chance to get pregnant," he said.

"My heart is divided into a million pieces," he said.

WHITE PHOSPHORUS

Al Jazeera Arabic shared video footage which appears to show a white phosphorus bomb being used in an attack on southern Lebanon.

Human Rights Watch had previously accused Israeli forces in October of using white phosphorus munitions in Lebanon and Gaza, which Israel denied.

White phosphorus is a wax-like, toxic substance that burns at nearly 1,500 degrees fahrenheit. It is hot enough to melt metal, burn skin down to the bone, and its chemical ingredients can be absorbed by the body, causing dysfunction in multiple organs, including the liver, kidneys and heart.

Harold Jaffe

IMPUNITY

The US state department has failed to act on internal reports of human rights abuses by Israeli army and police units, raising renewed questions over whether Washington's continued supply of arms to Israel is breaking US law.

The ProPublica Investigative Journalism site quoted officials as saying that a special panel set up by the Biden administration recommended that multiple Israeli military and police units be denied US funding because of serious human rights abuses. But the state department has yet to act on the recommendations.

The incidents mostly took place in the West Bank before the October 7 Hamas attack and the outbreak of the Gaza war. They included a case in which an elderly Palestinian-American man was gagged, handcuffed and left to die, and an allegation that interrogators tortured and raped a teenager accused of throwing rocks.

Joe Biden set up another mechanism in August last year for monitoring civilian casualties around the world caused by US-supplied weapons, in what was billed as an important new human rights safeguard. But the system, Civilian Harm Incident Response Guidance (CHIRG), has been run by just a half-dozen staffers working on it part-time.

Josh Paul, a former state dept official, said: "I am deeply skeptical that the administration is paying these issues the attention they deserve. There's such a culture of impunity that has developed where Israeli soldiers feel free to act without any concern of repercussions."

ISRAEL STRIKES BACK

Explosions echoed over an Iranian city on Friday in what sources described as an Israeli attack, but Tehran played down the incident and indicated it had no plans for retaliation.

The limited scale of the attack and Iran's muted response appeared to signal a successful effort by diplomats who have been working to avert all-out war since an Iranian drone and missile attack on Israel last Saturday.

Iranian media and officials described a small number of explosions, which they said resulted from air defenses hitting three drones over the city of Isfahan in central Iran. They referred to the incident as an attack by "infiltrators," rather than by Israel.

A senior Iranian official told Reuters there were no plans to respond against Israel.

What is new and dangerous, regardless of the scale or the posturing on both sides, is that a "new normal" is establishing itself in the conflict between Iran and Israel.

QUANTUM

Data from the UN shows that fewer than half of the required 500 trucks of aid a day are reaching Gaza. Aid groups have blamed Israeli restrictions for the holdup of trucks.

The secretary general, Antonio Guterres, said: "Apparent progress in one area is often cancelled out by delays and restrictions elsewhere. To avert imminent famine and further preventable deaths from disease,
>   We need a quantum leap in humanitarian aid to Palestinians in Gaza."

INTERNATIONAL ACTIVISTS

This week a group of international activists said they planned to sail from Turkey to Gaza on a flotilla of three ships carrying aid, a repeat of a 2010 effort that resulted in the death of nine activists and upended Turkish relations with Israel.

They intend to deliver ambulances, anesthesia and other items prevented from entering by enhanced restrictions on top of the 16-year Israeli blockade of Gaza. One of the activists, Huwaida Arraf, said the group members planned to protect themselves by broadcasting their whereabouts during the journey and training in non-violent methods of self-defense in case Israeli forces boarded the boats, as occurred in 2010.

Participants in the flotilla include international civil society groups as well as Turkey's Humanitarian Relief Foundation (İHH), whose head, Bülent Yıldırım, said there was "no choice" but to attempt another flotilla to Gaza.

Yıldırım and members of İHH were onboard a similar flotilla in 2010, which was boarded by Israeli commandos in international waters as it attempted to reach Gaza and murdered nine activists. most of them Turkish.

Activists onboard the current flotilla were reluctant to say where they intended to dock if they reached the territory, or how they might protect themselves while distributing aid. A recent Israeli attack on a convoy from the relief charity World Central Kitchen killed seven humanitarian workers.

Aid groups working in Gaza have criticized Washington's efforts to build a floating dock off the coast. Aid arriving overland has long proved to be the most effective at reaching those in need.

"We are doing what our governments should be doing, which is challenging Israel's conduct and policies," Arraf said.

Harold Jaffe

THE ISSUE FOR ISRAEL

is that while it anticipated the multi-front battles it would confront, the reality of fighting them has been confounding and draining on resources, both military and social.

The indiscriminate, even genocidal way Israel has fought since October 7 has also corroded and depleted its international support.

Even as its allies were stepping up to help it defend itself against Iran, the US and Europe were drawing up new sanctions to punish extremist settlers, with every indication of more to come.

In a messy, metastasizing conflict, whose objectives have become ever more unclear, observers are no longer asking whether Israel has the capacity to fight on multiple fronts. The actual question is: to what purpose? And at what ultimate cost?

TERRORIST MONSTERS

A unit of the Israel Defense Forces is facing US sanctions over its treatment of Palestinians in the occupied West Bank, even as Congress voted for $26bn in new emergency aid to Israel. *Even as Congress voted for $26bn in new emergency aid to Israel.*

The US state department say they are preparing to impose sanctions on the IDF's Netzah Yehuda battalion, which has been accused of serious human rights violations against Palestinians. Set up in 1999 to accommodate the religious beliefs of recruits from the ultra-Orthodox communities, the Netzah Yehuda battalion includes soldiers from extremist settlements.
	A unit from the battalion was accused in the death of a 78-year-old US citizen, Omar Assad, who died of a heart attack in 2022 after being detained, bound, gagged and abandoned.

The report that an IDF battalion is facing imminent sanctions prompted a sharp response from Benjamin Netanyahu.

"At a time when our soldiers are fighting terrorist monsters, the intention to issue sanctions against a unit in the IDF is the height of absurdity and a moral low."

Harold Jaffe

ABOUT TWO HOURS NORTH

As Israel expands its war on Gaza into a seventh month, about two hours north it has been fighting a parallel war along the border with Lebanon that threatens a wider regional conflict.

Since October 8, when Hezbollah launched attacks on Israel in solidarity with the Palestinian people, Israel has attacked it nearly 4,000 times along the 120km border.

Hezbollah was formed in 1982 to fight Israel's invasion and occupation of southern Lebanon. In 2006, the group fought a 34-day war widely regarded as a strategic and military failure for Israel.

Hezbollah chief Hassan Nasrallah has stopped short of declaring an all-out war against Israel but said its military operations will continue until the Israeli assault on Gaza stops. In response, Israeli leaders vowed to forcibly remove Hezbollah from Lebanon's south.

According to the Armed Conflict Location and Event Data Project (ACLED), Israel, Hezbollah and other armed groups in Lebanon exchanged at least 4,733 attacks across the border from October 7, 2023 to March 15, 2024.

Israel conducted about 83 percent of these attacks, totaling 3,952, while Hezbollah and other armed groups were responsible for 781 attacks.

About 65 percent of all attacks were artillery or missile, 25 percent were air or drone strikes, and the remaining 10 percent were armed clashes, destruction of property, remote explosives or improvised explosive device (IEDs).

In addition to Hezbollah, other forces involved in attacks against Israel include the Lebanese al-Fajr Forces and Amal Movement, as well as Hamas's Qassam Brigades and Islamic Jihad's al-Quds Brigades, both armed wings of Palestinian groups that maintain a presence in Lebanon.

UNTITLED

Doctors in Gaza have saved a baby from the womb of her mother as she lay dying from head injuries sustained in an Israeli airstrike. The child was delivered via an emergency caesarean section at a hospital in Rafah.

Sabreen al-Sakani, was 30 weeks pregnant when her family home was hit by an airstrike. Her husband, Shoukri, and their three-year-old daughter, Malak, also died.

"We managed to save the baby," Ahmad Fawzi al-Muqayyad, a doctor at the Kuwaiti hospital in Rafah, said.

"The mother was in a very critical condition. Her brain was exposed, so we saved one of the two."

On Sunday the baby lay wriggling and crying in an incubator in the neonatal unit of the nearby Emirati hospital.

The tag around her wrist bore her dead mother's name.

The baby's grandmother Mirvat al-Sakani told Associated Press that she would take care of her.

She is a memory of her father.

The Infected Desert

I will take care of her, she said.

My son was also with them.

My son became body parts and they have not found him yet.

They have nothing to do with anything.

Why are they targeting them?

We don't know why, how? We do not know.

WORLD COURT

Israel was ordered by the World Court on Friday to halt its military assault on the city of Rafah during the Gaza war.

Israel's far-right national security minister, Itamar Ben-Gvir's response was to quote Israel's first PM, David Ben-Gurion: "Our future is not dependent on what the gentiles will say but rather what the Jews will do!"

TWO SURPRISE ASSAULTS

It turns out that Hamas was not on its last legs after all. For the first time in months Hamas launched a barrage of rockets at Tel Aviv, which according to Israel did minimal damage.

Israel's relentless response only hours after was not really a surprise as they bombed a tent camp housing displaced people in a designated safe zone in Rafah killing at least 45 Palestinians, many of whom were women and children burned alive as the shelters caught fire.

Health officials in Gaza said the death toll was likely to rise as more people caught in the blaze were in critical condition with severe burns.

The attack on the tent camp in Tal as-Sultan came after Israeli forces bombed shelters housing displaced Palestinians in other areas, including Jabalia, Nuseirat and Gaza City, killing at least 160 civilians, according to Palestinian officials.

Balakrishnan Rajagopal, the UN special rapporteur on the right to housing, has called for action against Israel in the wake of its latest attack on displaced Palestinians in Rafah.

"Attacking women and children while they cower in their shelters in Rafah is a monstrous atrocity. We need concerted global action to stop Israel's actions now."

PARIAH

In the US, Republican congress-people along with mainstream media are uncovering anti-Semitism that isn't there while denouncing student protesters, faculty, administrators, and journalists for arguing on behalf of Palestine and peace in the Middle East.

Meanwhile, to Israel's chagrin, Spain, Ireland, and Norway have "formally" recognized the state of Palestine.

"In the midst of a war, with tens of thousands killed and injured, we must keep alive the only alternative that offers a political solution for Israelis and Palestinians alike: two states, living side by side, in peace and security," said Norway's prime minister.

Internationally, Israel now appears closer to what the former prime minister Ehud Barak called a "diplomatic tsunami" than any time in recent memory.

THE SAMSON OPTION*

The political scientist Norman Finkelstein asserts that before and especially after the October 8 attack, the Jewish state of Israel has been comprised of lunatics and pretended lunatics to terrify other countries, especially with Israel's inclination—or pretended inclination—to use nuclear weapons. Finkelstein maintains that Israel will keep escalating the provocations toward Iran and any other Muslim state—as it did to Egypt under Nasser and to the PLO under Arafat--to fight a massive war, possibly with Israel's nuclear arsenal. And ideally it will be a massive war that will drag countries such as the US, UK, France, and others into it.

*Title of a book by Seymour Hersh, 1991

Gratitude to the following news sites I've consulted from which I have sometimes borrowed and amended data.

Al Jazeera

The Guardian

The Intercept

Jacobin

Reuters

Scheerpost

Haaretz

Le Monde

The Irish Times

Jewish Insider

Zeteo

Special thanks to Susan Grace for reading this volume in ms and providing valuable comments.

ABOUT THE AUTHOR

Harold Jaffe is generally considered one of the foremost innovative writers in the US. His many books include fiction, "docufiction," drama and poetry, and several have been translated into French, German, Japanese, and Turkish. Representative titles are: PERFORMANCES FOR THE END OF TIME; 15 SERIAL KILLERS; SACRIFICE; EROS ANTI-EROS; SACRED ABJECT; DEATH CAFE; and TERROR-DOT-GOV.

Checklist of Previous JEF Titles

* Winners of the Kenneth Patchen Award for the Innovative Novel

- ☐ 0   *Projections* by Eckhard Gerdes
- ☐ 2   *Ring in a River* by Eckhard Gerdes
- ☐ 3   *The Darkness Starts Up Where You Stand* by Arthur Winfield Knight
- ☐ 4   *Belighted Fiction*
- ☐ 5   *Othello Blues* by Harold Jaffe
- ☐ 9   *Recto & Verso: A Work of Asemism and Pareidolia* by Dominic Ward & Eckhard Gerdes (Fridge Magnet Edition)
- ☐ 9B   *Recto & Verso: A Work of Asemism and Pareidolia* by Dominic Ward & Eckhard Gerdes (Trade Edition)
- ☐ 11   *Sore Eel Cheese* by The Flakxus Group (Limited Edition of 25)
- ☐ 14   *Writing Pictures: Case Studies in Photographic Criticism 1983-2012* by James R. Hugunin
- ☐ 15   *Wreck and Ruin: Photography, Temporality, and World(Dis)order* by James R. Hugunin
- ☐ 17   *John Barth, Bearded Bards & Splitting Hairs*
- ☐ 18   *99 Waves* by Persis Gerdes
- ☐ 22   *The Chronicles of Michel du Jabot* by Eckhard Gerdes
- ☐ 23   *The Laugh that Laughs at the Laugh: Writing from and about the Pen Man, Raymond Federman*
- ☐ 24   *A-Way with it!: Contemporary Innovative Fiction*
- ☐ 28   *Paris 60* by Harold Jaffe
- ☐ 29   *The Literary Terrorism of Harold Jaffe*
- ☐ 33   *Apostrophe/Parenthesis* by Frederick Mark Kramer
- ☐ 34   *Journal of Experimental Fiction 34: Foremost Fiction: A Report from the Front Lines*
- ☐ 35   *Journal of Experimental Fiction 35*
- ☐ 36   *Scuff Mud* (cd)
- ☐ 37   *Bizarro Fiction: Journal of Experimental Fiction 37*
- ☐ 38   *ATTOHO #1* (cd-r)
- ☐ 39   *Journal of Experimental Fiction 39*
- ☐ 40   *Ambiguity* by Frederick Mark Kramer

	41	*Prism and Graded Monotony* by Dominic Ward
☐	41	*Prism and Graded Monotony* by Dominic Ward
☐	42	*Short Tails* by Yuriy Tarnawsky
☐	43	*Something Is Crook in Middlebrook* by James R. Hugunin
☐	44	*Xanthous Mermaid Mechanics* by Brion Poloncic
☐	45	*OD: Docufictions* by Harold Jaffe
☐	46	*How to Break Article Noun* by Carolyn Chun*
☐	47	*Collected Stort Shories* by Eric Belgum
☐	48	*What Is Art?* by Norman Conquest
☐	49	*Don't Sing Aloha When I Go* by Robert Casella
☐	50	*Journal of Experimental Fiction 50*
☐	51	*Oppression for the Heaven of It* by Moore Bowen*
☐	52	*Elder Physics* by James R. Hugunin
☐	53.1	*Like Blood in Water: Five Mininovels (The Placebo Effect Trilogy #1)* by Yuriy Tarnawsky
☐	53.2	*The Future of Giraffes: Five Mininovels (The Placebo Effect Trilogy #2)* by Yuriy Tarnawsky
☐	53.3	*View of Delft: Five Mininovels (The Placebo Effect Trilogy #3)* by Yuriy Tarnawsky
☐	54	*You Are Make Very Important Bathtime* by David Moscovich
☐	55	*Minnows: A Shattered Novel* by Jønathan Lyons
☐	56	*Meanwhile* by Frederick Mark Kramer
☐	58A	*Tar Spackled Banner* by James R. Hugunin
☐	58B	*Return to Circa '96* by Bob Sawatzki*
☐	60	*Case X* by James R. Hugunin
☐	61	*Naked Lunch at Tiffany's* by Derek Pell
☐	62	*Tangled in Motion* by Jane L. Carman
☐	64	*The Hunter* by Dominic Ward
☐	65	*A Little Story about Maurice Ravel* by Conger Beasley, Jr.
☐	66	*Psychedelic Everest* by Brion Poloncic
☐	67	*Between the Legs* by Kate Horsley*
☐	68	*Claim to Oblivion: Selected Essays and Interviews* by Yuriy Tarnawsky
☐	69	*Passions and Shadows or Shadows and Passions* by Frederick Mark Kramer

	70	*Afterimage: Critical Essays on Photography* by James R. Hugunin
☐	71	*Goosestep* by Harold Jaffe
☐	72	*Science Fiction: A Poem!* by Robin Wyatt Dunne
☐	73	*Offbeat/Quirky*
☐	74	*Mouth* by Charles Hood*
☐	75	*Q ↔A* by James R. Hugunin
☐	76	*Literary Yoga* by Yuriy Tarnawsky
☐	77	*Experimental Literature: A Collection of Statements* edited by Jeffrey R. Di Leo and Warren Motte
☐	78	*The Skrat Prize Memorial Anthology* by R.M. Strauss*
☐	79	*Black Scat Books: A Bibliography 2012 – 2018* compiled by Grace Murray
☐	80	*Finding Mememo* by James R. Hugunin
☐	81	*Porn-anti-Porn* by Harold Jaffe
☐	82	*Understanding Franklin Thompson* by Jim Meirose
☐	83	*Warm Arctic Nights* by Yuriy Tarnawsky
☐	84	*The Iguanas of Heat* by Yuriy Tarnawsky
☐	85	*Death at Half Mast* by Denis Emorine
☐	86	*Those Brave As the Skate Is* by Patrick Keller*
☐	87	*The Marble Corridor* by Ryan Madej
☐	88	*Crocodile Smiles* by Yuriy Tarnawsky
☐	89	*Plague City* by Genelle Chaconas*
☐	90	*Picky Hunting* by James R. Hugunin
☐	91	*"The Greatest Place on Earth": A Personal Note: A Work of Absurdity?* by Jeff Weisman
☐	92	*Own Little Worlds* by Cal Massey*
☐	93	*Picky Unchained* by James R. Hugunin
☐	94	*Picky's Constant Conversation* by James R. Hugunin
☐	95	*A is for Alphabet* by Dennis Vanderspek*
☐	96	*MOFA: The Museum of Fungible Art* by Norman Conquest
☐	97	*The Makings of a Nobody: A Fictmoir* by Ann Z. Leventhal*
☐	98	*Polyphony*
☐	99	*Out of Competition* by Lew Collins*

www.ingramcontent.com/pod-product-compliance
Lightning Source LLC
Chambersburg PA
CBHW030044100526
44590CB00011B/325